TENOR SAX

101 BROADWAY SONGS

Note: The keys in this book do not match the other wind instruments.

Available for
FLUTE, CLARINET, ALTO SAX, TENOR SAX, TRUMPET,
HORN, TROMBONE, VIOLIN, VIOLA, CELLO

ISBN 978-1-4950-5249-1

Visit Hal Leonard Online at
www.halleonard.com

Contact us:
Hal Leonard
7777 West Bluemound Road
Milwaukee, WI 53213
Email: info@halleonard.com

In Europe, contact:
Hal Leonard Europe Limited
42 Wigmore Street
Marylebone, London, W1U 2RN
Email: info@halleonardeurope.com

In Australia, contact:
Hal Leonard Australia Pty. Ltd.
4 Lentara Court
Cheltenham, Victoria, 3192 Australia
Email: info@halleonard.com.au

CONTENTS

ALL I ASK OF YOU
from THE PHANTOM OF THE OPERA

TENOR SAX

Music by ANDREW LLOYD WEBBER
Lyrics by CHARLES HART
Additional Lyrics by RICHARD STILGOE

Moderately slow

ANY DREAM WILL DO

from JOSEPH AND THE AMAZING TECHNICOLOR® DREAMCOAT

TENOR SAX

Music by ANDREW LLOYD WEBBER
Lyrics by TIM RICE

ANYTHING YOU CAN DO

from the Stage Production ANNIE GET YOUR GUN

TENOR SAX

Words and Music by
IRVING BERLIN

AS IF WE NEVER SAID GOODBYE

from SUNSET BOULEVARD

TENOR SAX

Music by ANDREW LLOYD WEBBER
Lyrics by DON BLACK and CHRISTOPHER HAMPTON,
with contributions by AMY POWERS

AS LONG AS HE NEEDS ME

from the Broadway Musical OLIVER!

TENOR SAX

Words and Music by
LIONEL BART

BALI HA'I
from SOUTH PACIFIC

TENOR SAX

Lyrics by OSCAR HAMMERSTEIN II
Music by RICHARD RODGERS

BAUBLES, BANGLES AND BEADS

from KISMET

TENOR SAX

Words and Music by ROBERT WRIGHT
and GEORGE FORREST
(Music Based on Themes of A. BORODIN)

BROTHERHOOD OF MAN

from HOW TO SUCCEED IN BUSINESS WITHOUT REALLY TRYING

TENOR SAX

By FRANK LOESSER

CABARET
from the Musical CABARET

TENOR SAX

Words by FRED EBB
Music by JOHN KANDER

CAN'T TAKE MY EYES OFF OF YOU

featured in JERSEY BOYS

TENOR SAX

Words and Music by BOB CREWE
and BOB GAUDIO

CIRCLE OF LIFE

Disney Presents THE LION KING: THE BROADWAY MUSICAL

TENOR SAX

Music by ELTON JOHN
Lyrics by TIM RICE

Moderately, with an African beat

CLIMB EV'RY MOUNTAIN

from THE SOUND OF MUSIC

TENOR SAX

Lyrics by OSCAR HAMMERSTEIN II
Music by RICHARD RODGERS

Majestically

CLOSE EVERY DOOR

from JOSEPH AND THE AMAZING TECHNICOLOR® DREAMCOAT

TENOR SAX

Music by ANDREW LLOYD WEBBER
Lyrics by TIM RICE

Moderately, expressively

DANCING QUEEN

from MAMMA MIA!

TENOR SAX

Words and Music by BENNY ANDERSSON,
BJÖRN ULVAEUS and STIG ANDERSON

DEFYING GRAVITY

from the Broadway Musical WICKED

TENOR SAX

Music and Lyrics by
STEPHEN SCHWARTZ

Tempo I

DO-RE-MI
from THE SOUND OF MUSIC

TENOR SAX

Lyrics by OSCAR HAMMERSTEIN II
Music by RICHARD RODGERS

DO YOU HEAR THE PEOPLE SING?

from LES MISÉRABLES

TENOR SAX

Music by CLAUDE-MICHEL SCHÖNBERG
Lyrics by ALAIN BOUBLIL, JEAN-MARC NATEL
and HERBERT KRETZMER

DON'T CRY FOR ME ARGENTINA
from EVITA

TENOR SAX

Words by TIM RICE
Music by ANDREW LLOYD WEBBER

EASTER PARADE

from AS THOUSANDS CHEER

TENOR SAX

Words and Music by
IRVING BERLIN

EDELWEISS
from THE SOUND OF MUSIC

TENOR SAX

Lyrics by OSCAR HAMMERSTEIN II
Music by RICHARD RODGERS

EVERYTHING'S ALRIGHT

from JESUS CHRIST SUPERSTAR

Tenor Sax

Words by TIM RICE
Music by ANDREW LLOYD WEBBER

A FOGGY DAY (IN LONDON TOWN)

from A DAMSEL IN DISTRESS

Tenor Sax

Music and Lyrics by GEORGE GERSHWIN
and IRA GERSHWIN

GETTING TO KNOW YOU

from THE KING AND I

TENOR SAX

Lyrics by OSCAR HAMMERSTEIN II
Music by RICHARD RODGERS

FRIEND LIKE ME
(Stageplay Version)
from the Walt Disney Stageplay ALADDIN

TENOR SAX

Music by ALAN MENKEN
Lyrics by HOWARD ASHMAN
and STEPHEN SCHWARTZ

GUYS AND DOLLS

from GUYS AND DOLLS

TENOR SAX

By FRANK LOESSER

HELLO, DOLLY!

from HELLO, DOLLY!

TENOR SAX

Music and Lyric by
JERRY HERMAN

HOME

from Walt Disney's BEAUTY AND THE BEAST: THE BROADWAY MUSICAL

TENOR SAX

Music by ALAN MENKEN
Lyrics by TIM RICE

HOW ARE THINGS IN GLOCCA MORRA
from FINIAN'S RAINBOW

TENOR SAX

Words by E.Y. "YIP" HARBURG
Music by BURTON LANE

Slowly

I BELIEVE IN YOU

from HOW TO SUCCEED IN BUSINESS WITHOUT REALLY TRYING

TENOR SAX

By FRANK LOESSER

I DON'T KNOW HOW TO LOVE HIM

from JESUS CHRIST SUPERSTAR

Tenor Sax

Words by TIM RICE
Music by ANDREW LLOYD WEBBER

I DREAMED A DREAM

from LES MISÉRABLES

TENOR SAX

Music by CLAUDE-MICHEL SCHÖNBERG
Lyrics by ALAIN BOUBLIL, JEAN-MARC NATEL
and HERBERT KRETZMER

I GOT PLENTY O' NUTTIN'

from PORGY AND BESS®

TENOR SAX

Music and Lyrics by GEORGE GERSHWIN,
DuBOSE and DORTHY HEYWARD
and IRA GERSHWIN

I WHISTLE A HAPPY TUNE

from THE KING AND I

TENOR SAX

Lyrics by OSCAR HAMMERSTEIN II
Music by RICHARD RODGERS

Brightly

I'VE NEVER BEEN IN LOVE BEFORE

from GUYS AND DOLLS

TENOR SAX

By FRANK LOESSER

IF I LOVED YOU

from CAROUSEL

TENOR SAX

Lyrics by OSCAR HAMMERSTEIN II
Music by RICHARD RODGERS

Slowly

IF I WERE A BELL

from GUYS AND DOLLS

TENOR SAX

By FRANK LOESSER

IF I WERE A RICH MAN

from the Musical FIDDLER ON THE ROOF

Tenor Sax

Words by SHELDON HARNICK
Music by JERRY BOCK

THE IMPOSSIBLE DREAM
(The Quest)
from MAN OF LA MANCHA

TENOR SAX

Lyric by JOE DARION
Music by MITCH LEIGH

IT AIN'T NECESSARILY SO

from PORGY AND BESS®

TENOR SAX

Music and Lyrics by GEORGE GERSHWIN,
DuBOSE and DOROTHY HEYWARD
and IRA GERSHWIN

THE LADY IS A TRAMP

from BABES IN ARMS

TENOR SAX

Words by LORENZ HART
Music by RICHARD RODGERS

THE LAST NIGHT OF THE WORLD

from MISS SAIGON

TENOR SAX

Music by CLAUDE-MICHEL SCHÖNBERG
Lyrics by ALAIN BOUBLIL and RICHARD MALTBY JR.
Adapted from original French Lyrics by ALAIN BOUBLIL

LET'S CALL THE WHOLE THING OFF

from SHALL WE DANCE

TENOR SAX

Music and Lyrics by GEORGE GERSHWIN
and IRA GERSHWIN

LOVE IS HERE TO STAY

from GOLDWYN FOLLIES

TENOR SAX

Music and Lyrics by GEORGE GERSHWIN
and IRA GERSHWIN

Medium Swing

LOVE ME OR LEAVE ME

from WHOOPEE!

Tenor Sax

Lyrics by GUS KAHN
Music by WALTER DONALDSON

LOVE WALKED IN
from GOLDWYN FOLLIES

TENOR SAX

Music and Lyrics by GEORGE GERSHWIN
and IRA GERSHWIN

LUCK BE A LADY
from GUYS AND DOLLS

TENOR SAX

By FRANK LOESSER

MAKIN' WHOOPEE!

from WHOOPEE!

Tenor Sax

Lyrics by GUS KAHN
Music by WALTER DONALDSON

MAME
from MAME

TENOR SAX

Music and Lyric by
JERRY HERMAN

MAMMA MIA
from MAMMA MIA!

Tenor Sax

Words and Music by BENNY ANDERSSON,
BJÖRN ULVAEUS and STIG ANDERSON

MATCHMAKER
from the Musical FIDDLER ON THE ROOF

TENOR SAX

Words by SHELDON HARNICK
Music by JERRY BOCK

MAYBE
from the Musical Production ANNIE

Lyric by MARTIN CHARNIN
Music by CHARLES STROUSE

Tenor Sax

MEMORY

from CATS

TENOR SAX

Music by ANDREW LLOYD WEBBER
Text by TREVOR NUNN after T.S. ELIOT

THE MUSIC OF THE NIGHT
from THE PHANTOM OF THE OPERA

TENOR SAX

Music by ANDREW LLOYD WEBBER
Lyrics by CHARLES HART
Additional Lyrics by RICHARD STILGOE

MY FAVORITE THINGS

from THE SOUND OF MUSIC

TENOR SAX

Lyrics by OSCAR HAMMERSTEIN II
Music by RICHARD RODGERS

NICE WORK IF YOU CAN GET IT

from A DAMSEL IN DISTRESS

Tenor Sax

Music and Lyrics by GEORGE GERSHWIN
and IRA GERSWIN

OH, WHAT A BEAUTIFUL MORNIN'

from OKLAHOMA!

TENOR SAX

Lyrics by OSCAR HAMMERSTEIN II
Music by RICHARD RODGERS

OKLAHOMA
from OKLAHOMA!

TENOR SAX

Lyrics by OSCAR HAMMERSTEIN II
Music by RICHARD RODGERS

OL' MAN RIVER

from SHOW BOAT

TENOR SAX

Lyrics by OSCAR HAMMERSTEIN II
Music by JEROME KERN

OLD DEVIL MOON
from FINIAN'S RAINBOW

Tenor Sax

Words by E.Y. "YIP" HARBURG
Music by BURTON LANE

ON MY OWN

from LES MISÉRABLES

TENOR SAX

Music by CLAUDE-MICHEL SCHÖNBERG
Lyrics by ALAIN BOUBLIL, JEAN-MARC NATEL,
HERBERT KRETZMER, JOHN CAIRD
and TREVOR NUNN

Moderately slow

ONCE IN A LIFETIME

from the Musical Production STOP THE WORLD—I WANT TO GET OFF

Tenor Sax

Words and Music by LESLIE BRICUSSE
and ANTHONY NEWLEY

ONCE IN LOVE WITH AMY

from WHERE'S CHARLEY?

Tenor Sax

By FRANK LOESSER

ONE
from A CHORUS LINE

Tenor Sax

Music by MARVIN HAMLISCH
Lyric by EDWARD KLEBAN

PEOPLE WILL SAY WE'RE IN LOVE

from OKLAHOMA!

TENOR SAX

Lyrics by OSCAR HAMMERSTEIN II
Music by RICHARD RODGERS

THE PHANTOM OF THE OPERA

from THE PHANTOM OF THE OPERA

Tenor Sax

Music by ANDREW LLOYD WEBBER
Lyrics by CHARLES HART
Additional Lyrics by RICHARD STILGOE
and MIKE BATT

Moderately fast

POPULAR
from the Broadway Musical WICKED

TENOR SAX

Music and Lyrics by
STEPHEN SCHWARTZ

SEASONS OF LOVE

from RENT

TENOR SAX

Words and Music by
JONATHAN LARSON

SEND IN THE CLOWNS

from the Musical A LITTLE NIGHT MUSIC

TENOR SAX

Words and Music by
STEPHEN SONDHEIM

SEVENTY SIX TROMBONES

from Meredith Willson's THE MUSIC MAN

TENOR SAX

By MEREDITH WILLSON

SHALL WE DANCE?

from THE KING AND I

TENOR SAX

Lyrics by OSCAR HAMMERSTEIN II
Music by RICHARD RODGERS

SHE LOVES ME
from SHE LOVES ME

TENOR SAX

Words by SHELDON HARNICK
Music by JERRY BOCK

SHERRY
featured in JERSEY BOYS

TENOR SAX

Words and Music by
BOB GAUDIO

SOME ENCHANTED EVENING

from SOUTH PACIFIC

TENOR SAX

Lyrics by OSCAR HAMMERSTEIN II
Music by RICHARD RODGERS

SUMMERTIME

from PORGY AND BESS®

TENOR SAX

Music and Lyrics by GEORGE GERSHWIN,
DuBOSE and DOROTHY HEYWARD
and IRA GERSHWIN

SUNRISE, SUNSET

from the Musical FIDDLER ON THE ROOF

Tenor Sax

Words by SHELDON HARNICK
Music by JERRY BOCK

Moderately slow Waltz

SUPERSTAR
from JESUS CHRIST SUPERSTAR

TENOR SAX

Words by TIM RICE
Music by ANDREW LLOYD WEBBER

THE SURREY WITH THE FRINGE ON TOP

from OKLAHOMA!

TENOR SAX

Lyrics by OSCAR HAMMERSTEIN II
Music by RICHARD RODGERS

THE SWEETEST SOUNDS

from NO STRINGS

TENOR SAX

Lyrics and Music by
RICHARD RODGERS

THERE'S NO BUSINESS LIKE SHOW BUSINESS

from the Stage Production ANNIE GET YOUR GUN

TENOR SAX

Words and Music by
IRVING BERLIN

THEY ALL LAUGHED

from SHALL WE DANCE

TENOR SAX

Music and Lyrics by GEORGE GERSHWIN
and IRA GERSHWIN

THEY CAN'T TAKE THAT AWAY FROM ME

from SHALL WE DANCE

Tenor Sax

Music and Lyrics by GEORGE GERSHWIN
and IRA GERSHWIN

THINK OF ME

from THE PHANTOM OF THE OPERA

TENOR SAX

Music by ANDREW LLOYD WEBBER
Lyrics by CHARLES HART
Additional Lyrics by RICHARD STILGOE

THIS IS THE MOMENT

from JEKYLL & HYDE

TENOR SAX

Words and Music by LESLIE BRICUSSE
and FRANK WILDHORN

THIS NEARLY WAS MINE

from SOUTH PACIFIC

TENOR SAX

Lyrics by OSCAR HAMMERSTEIN II
Music by RICHARD RODGERS

TILL THERE WAS YOU

from Meredith Willson's THE MUSIC MAN

TENOR SAX

By MEREDITH WILLSON

TOMORROW
from the Musical Production ANNIE

TENOR SAX

Lyric by MARTIN CHARNIN
Music by CHARLES STROUSE

WALK LIKE A MAN

featured in *JERSEY BOYS*

TENOR SAX

Words and Music by BOB CREWE
and BOB GAUDIO

UNUSUAL WAY

from NINE

TENOR SAX

Music and Lyrics by
MAURY YESTON

WHAT I DID FOR LOVE
from A CHORUS LINE

TENOR SAX

Music by MARVIN HAMLISCH
Lyric by EDWARD KLEBAN

WHAT KIND OF FOOL AM I?

from the Musical Production STOP THE WORLD—I WANT TO GET OFF

TENOR SAX

Words and Music by LESLIE BRICUSSE
and ANTHONY NEWLEY

WHERE IS LOVE?

from the Broadway Musical OLIVER!

TENOR SAX

Words and Music by
LIONEL BART

WHO CAN I TURN TO

(When Nobody Needs Me)

from THE ROAR OF THE GREASEPAINT—THE SMELL OF THE CROWD

Tenor Sax

Words and Music by LESLIE BRICUSSE
and ANTHONY NEWLEY

Slowly

A WHOLE NEW WORLD

from the Walt Disney Stageplay ALADDIN

TENOR SAX

Music by ALAN MENKEN
Lyrics by TIM RICE

WILL YOU LOVE ME TOMORROW
(Will You Still Love Me Tomorrow)
from BEAUTIFUL

Tenor Sax

Words and Music by GERRY GOFFIN
and CAROLE KING

WITH ONE LOOK

from SUNSET BOULEVARD

TENOR SAX

Music by ANDREW LLOYD WEBBER
Lyrics by DON BLACK and CHRISTOPHER HAMPTON,
with contributions by AMY POWERS

WRITTEN IN THE STARS

from Elton John and Tim Rice's AIDA

TENOR SAX

Music by ELTON JOHN
Lyrics by TIM RICE

YOU RULE MY WORLD

from THE FULL MONTY

TENOR SAX

Words and Music by
DAVID YAZBEK

YOU'LL NEVER WALK ALONE
from CAROUSEL

Tenor Sax

Lyrics by OSCAR HAMMERSTEIN II
Music by RICHARD RODGERS

YOU'LL BE IN MY HEART

Disney Presents TARZAN The Broadway Musical

TENOR SAX

Words and Music by
PHIL COLLINS

D.S. al Coda

CODA

YOU'VE GOT A FRIEND
from BEAUTIFUL

TENOR SAX

Words and Music by
CAROLE KING

YOUNGER THAN SPRINGTIME
from SOUTH PACIFIC

TENOR SAX

Lyrics by OSCAR HAMMERSTEIN II
Music by RICHARD RODGERS